4.95

Chinese

...stration

FRANCES WOOD

COLLEGE OF TECHNOLOGY

The British Library

or 7/93

BL

Front cover A keepsake from the cloud gallery. Large manuscript folio of *Yun tai xian rui* in concertina form containing illustrations with accompanying text. (See page 69.)

Back cover Colour print from the Ten Bamboo Studio, Nanjing, *c.* 1643. (See pages 64, 65.)

Published by
The British Library
Reference Division Publications
Great Russell Street
London WC1B 3DG

and 51 Washington Street,
Dover, New Hampshire 03820

British Library Cataloguing in Publication Data

Wood, Frances
   Chinese illustration.
   1. Illustration of books——China
   I. Title   II. British Library
   741.64'0951   NC990.5

   ISBN 0–7123–0053–8

Library of Congress Cataloging in Publication Data

Wood, Frances.
   Chinese Illustration.

   Bibliography: P.
   1. Illustration of books – China. 2.
Graphic arts – China. 3. Printing –
China – history. 4. British Library. I.
British Library. II. Title.
Library. II. Title.
NC990.5.W66   1985   741.6'0951
85–18989
   ISBN 0–7123–0053–8 (Pbk.)

Designed by Roger Davies
Typeset in Monophoto Ehrhardt by August Filmsetting,
Haydock, St Helens
Origination by York House Graphics, Hanwell
Printed in Great Britain by William Clowes Ltd, Beccles

Contents

Outer coat worn by a 5th
rank courtier. From a
manuscript album based on
the *Huang Chao li qi tu shi*.
(See page 44.)

Introduction

The history of illustration in China is almost the reverse of the European tradition, for printing – invented in China – begins to dominate at a very early stage. The starting point for book illustration in the West lies with the magnificently illuminated manuscripts first produced in the 5th century, a tradition of richly decorated individual items which continued into the the 15th century when printing arrived in Europe. In China, the same period saw the invention of printing, its growth into a massive industry supplying the court and gentry with fine editions and the ordinary city population with cheap illustrated novels, and, finally, the last great innovation in Chinese printing, the development of fine colour printing from multiple wood-blocks during the Ming period (AD 1368–1644).

Just as in Europe, manuscript production in China did not die out immediately printing was invented. In the 9th and 10th centuries, the two methods existed side by side, as can be seen in the great library discovered in the cave temples at Dunhuang on the Silk Road in the remote north-western province of Gansu. The library included the world's first printed 'book' – an illustrated Chinese translation of the Diamond sutra (AD 868) – and other illustrated printed items, together with thousands of manuscripts of Buddhist texts, some, like the illustrated Lotus sutra booklet, probably later than the Diamond sutra.

Later, though printing supplied an enormous market and colour-printed albums largely supplanted more expensive

one-off illustrated manuscripts, these continued to be produced for the court, for collectors, and, in the 18th and 19th centuries, for the growing export market to Europe. Nevertheless, the history of Chinese illustration, as we trace it in this book, is very much the history of printing in China and it begins with the Diamond sutra in 868, which is now in the British Library.

The British Library Chinese collection dates back to the first year of the British Museum, 1753, when three Chinese books were acquired as part of the Sloane collection. Further items were added from the Harleian, Old Royal and Lansdowne collections and, as British interests in the Far East expanded, residents abroad bequeathed collections. Five cases of Chinese books seized during the Opium War were donated by Queen Victoria in 1843. The most significant collection is that made by Stein in Dunhuang and other parts of Chinese Central Asia on his three expeditions (1900–1916), a vast archive which included the Diamond sutra and other illustrated Buddhist items dating from the 5th to the 10th centuries. The incorporation of the India Office Library into the British Library has brought in a small Chinese collection with some notable export paintings from the East India Company's factory in Canton. The collection continues to grow through purchase; among other items, the Qi sha tripitaka volume (9) and the Ming Buddhist booklet were acquired in 1983 and a collection of operatic 'New Year' prints in 1984.

著書
十竹齋寫

凡欲讀經先念淨口業真言□遍

褊唎　褊唎　摩訶褊唎

奉請除穢金剛

奉請白淨水金剛

奉請紫賢金剛

　　　　　　褊唎

　　　　　摩訶褊唎

奉請辟妻金剛

奉請赤聲金剛

奉請大神金剛

　　　　褊褊唎　婆婆訶

奉請黃隨求金剛

奉請定除尼金剛

金剛般若波羅蜜經

如是我聞一時佛在舍衛國祇樹給孤獨園與大
比丘衆千二百五十人俱尒時世尊食時著衣持
鉢入舍衛大城乞食於其城中次第乞已還至本處
飯食訖收衣鉢洗足已數座而坐時長老須菩提在大
衆中即從座起偏袒右肩右膝著地合掌恭敬而
白佛言希有世尊如来善護念諸菩薩善付囑諸菩

It seems likely that Buddhism, which views the distribution of texts and the duplication of images as devout works, played a part in the Chinese invention of printing, which is of its nature an act of duplication. There were, however, other elements in Chinese culture which helped its development. From the Shang dynasty (c 1700–1066 BC) seals, or 'chops', with personal names carved in them were used as stamps of authority, and during the Han (206 BC–AD 220) ink-rubbings were taken from stone inscriptions, inscriptions which had been carved as official and unalterable texts of, for example, the Confucian classics. These ink-rubbings (also made by Buddhists from stone-carved sutras from the mid-6th century) produced multiple copies but in a labour-intensive and painstaking manner more comparable with brass-rubbing than printing. Ink-rubbings were made possible by the invention of paper in the early Han; paper is an essential prerequisite for printing, for it is cheap to produce in the quantities necessary for large printed editions.

It is clear from the many thousands of paper manuscripts found at Dunhuang that paper was in widespread use by the 5th century and while the Diamond sutra (1) was not printed until 868, it is obvious from its quality that printing must have been developed well before that date – though the fragile nature of paper means that surviving examples are hard to find. The Diamond sutra is a woodblock print (2), a printing method most suitable to the Chinese script (which is non-alphabetic and comprises tens of thousands of different characters) and which readily combines text and illustration, either on separate blocks, as in the Diamond sutra, or on the same block (4, 6).

Many of the earliest surviving prints and manuscripts are religious, mostly Buddhist. This may be accidental, for the enormous library at Dunhuang which holds so many examples was perfectly preserved by climate and by human neglect. These religious books do, however, illustrate the development of the Chinese book from a scroll, through the 'sutra' (or concertina) binding, to the thread-bound book.

The examples with half-page illustrations also demonstrate the growth of a very popular form, later to be used for fiction, where text and illustration are combined. This combination, which makes the whole easier to read and understand, may have developed because of the nature of the Chinese language. With its potentially enormous vocabulary, there must have been very varying degrees of literacy, ranging from the scholar who had mastered up to 10,000 characters and would consult dictionaries readily, to people who had learned enough for daily use, in accounting and book-keeping for example, but whose restricted vocabulary of only a couple of hundred words would exclude them from learned works. They might well, however, be able to read short illustrated works.

1 The Diamond sutra.

Translation of the *Vajracchedikāprajñāpāramitāsūtra* into Chinese. Woodblock print in roll form with frontispiece found at Dunhuang. Colophon dated AD 868.

[Or.8210/P.2.]

The world's earliest printed 'book', the Diamond sutra consists of sheets of printed text stuck onto a backing and rolled into a scroll. This rolled format was a development from an earlier form of 'book' in which inscriptions, texts or records were written on long narrow strips of bamboo which were bound together by two strings so that they could be kept in order and rolled up for convenient storage. The format was retained for some time after the advent of paper, but was eventually replaced by the method by which pages are sewn in at the spine.

The Diamond sutra must represent a late stage in the development of printing for it is a considerable work, over 16 feet long. It has a wonderfully carved frontispiece of the Buddha sitting cross-legged on a lotus throne behind a small table, preaching to his aged disciple who sits on a mat, his shoes neatly placed beside him. At the time, the Chinese still sat on mats (a custom which was exported to Japan where it persists) for chairs were not used in China until the late 9th century. A crowd of monks surround the Buddha who, like his disciple wears monks' robes (made of squares of cloth, the squares outlined in black in this illustration). Above the head of the Buddha are a pair of apsareses (Buddhist 'angels') amongst clouds, on either side of a canopy hung with ropes of precious stones. On either side is a fierce guardian of the faith and a pair of a small lions, another protective symbol (although here looking more like cats in front of a fireplace). On the table are vessels of chased silver and an embroidered cloth and the whole floor seems to be covered in marvellously carved tiles (which were used in some early temples.)

The colophon, which dates this printing so accurately, reads: 'Reverently [caused to be] made for universal free distribution by Wang Jie on behalf of his parents on the 15th of the 4th moon of the 9th year of Xian tong [11th May, 868]'. The fact that he had it printed for free, and presumably wide, distribution as an act of merit on behalf of his parents strengthens the theory of the link between Buddhism and printing because it was of course possible to distribute so many more texts if they were printed.

2 Woodblock.
Carved with pages of the
'Impartial power' section of
the *Yin zhi jin jian* (A mirror
of hidden good).

Woodblocks such as this were
used to print Chinese texts
from at least the 9th century
and probably much earlier.
They were carved from
pearwood, jujube and catalpa,
all of which are smooth and
evenly textured. Pear and
jujube were most commonly
used for texts whilst catalpa,
which is harder, was more
suitable for the fine line of
illustration.

   This block is carved on
both sides, which was
common practise, and the
page format is clear. Two
pages of text are carved with
the margin in the middle.
When printed, the thin sheet
of paper was folded along the
central margin and the two
outer sides stitched into the
spine. The carving was done
from a thin sheet of
manuscript (or, in the case of
a reprint, a printed sheet
unstitched from the earlier
edition) which would have
been pasted face down on the
block. Where mistakes were
made in the cutting, the
characters would be cut out
and small replacements
inserted (see the space at the
top right of this block).

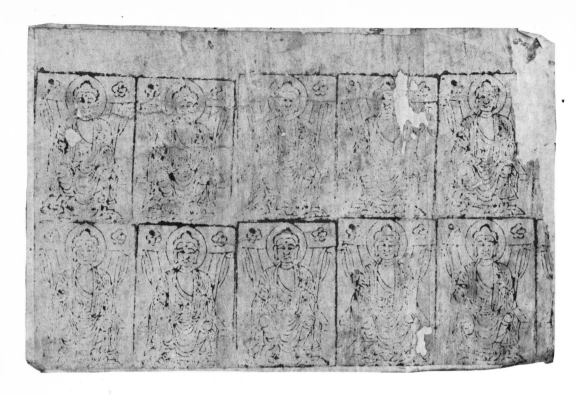

3 Stamped images of a seated Buddha.
Found at Dunhuang. ?8th century
AD. [Or.8210/p.18.]

Small stamped images such as these may have produced some of the impetus
for the development of printing in China. Though the Chinese had long been
using seals or 'chops' it was not until after the invention of paper during the
Han period that printing became a real possibility, so personal seals as such
may not have had much influence on the invention of printing. Monks at
Dunhuang used to paint hundreds of tiny Buddha figures as an act of devotion;
with the use of a small stamp, they could reproduce thousands, rather than
hundreds, in a day.

4 Printed prayer-sheet.
From Dunhuang. Prayer-sheet with illustration of Amitābha Buddha. Woodblock, 10th century.
[Or.8210/p.14.]

A large number of such printed prayer-sheets were found in the walled-up library at Dunhuang, and, though mostly undated, are amongst the earliest examples of printing found in China. Like the Diamond sutra, they were probably financed and printed by believers as an act of faith.

Amitābha, a very popular Buddha in China and, later, Japan, is depicted meditating on a lotus throne. Beneath him are prayers and the characters to his left read 'Universal exhortation to worship and maintenance of the faith', and those on the right, 'Amitābha Buddha of the 48 vows'. The most important of these vows is the 18th, in which Amitābha promises to refuse Buddha-hood until he has saved all living beings, except those who had committed the five unpardonable sins or were guilty of blasphemy. Amitābha presided over the Western Paradise which is, theoretically, only a stage on the journey to *nirvāna* but is traditionally assumed to be the final resting-place of those who have called his name. Memorial services in Buddhist temples today are followed by a shorter service in which all present call on Amitābha to take the deceased into his heaven.

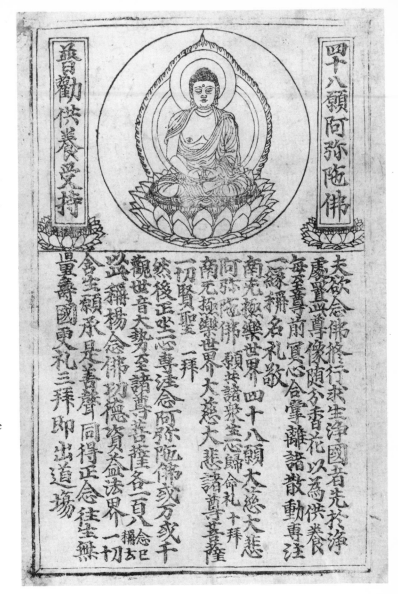

復加害
設復有人若有罪
若无罪杻械枷
鏁禁繫其身稱
觀世音菩薩名者

昏悉斷懷即得
解脫
若三千大千國土
滿中怨賊有一
商主将諸商

5 The Lotus sutra.

Manuscript booklet of chapter 25 with illustrations in ink and colour.
Dunhuang, 10th century.

[Or.8210/S.6983.]

The most popular chapter of the Lotus sutra was the 25th which extols the virtues of the Bodhisattva Guanyin (Sanskrit: Avalokiteśvara) whose full name in Chinese means 'The one who listens to the cries of the world'. The illustration on the right appears above a passage which says that, whether innocent or guilty, a person will lose his fetters if he calls upon Guanyin. The standing figure has a cangue around his neck – a wooden collar, rather like a personal version of the stocks, which was fastened onto criminals in China.

The format of the booklet is interesting as it anticipates an extremely popular printed form with half-page illustrations above the text which was used for novels, plays and popular works during the Ming (1368–1644).

6 Printed prayer-sheet.
From Dunhuang. Prayer-sheet with illustration of Mañjuśrī riding a lion. Woodblock, 9th or 10th century.

[Or.8210/p.5.]

Mañjuśrī was the Buddhists' guardian of wisdom and is also described in the Lotus sutra as the ninth Buddha-ancestor of Sakyamuni. He is usually depicted, as here, riding on a lion, the symbol of his stern majesty. Beneath Mañjuśrī and attendants are a short prayer and a *dhāraṇi* (incantation). On the left, the characters are identical with those on the prayer-sheet of Amitābha (4) and on the right they read 'The very holy Bodhisattva Mañjuśrī'.

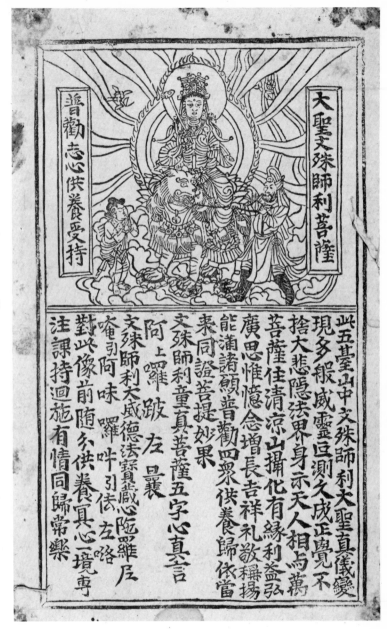

7 Sketches.

From the walled-up library at Dunhuang. Brush and ink sketches on the reverse of a fine manuscript of the Diamond sutra. Possibly 7th century.

[Or.8210/S.259.]

Though paper was widely used from the 5th century, it was still a fairly precious material and many fragments found at Dunhuang have been used and re-used. It is, however, unusual to find sketches on the back of a fine manuscript.

The sketches depict figures commonly found in the wall-paintings and banners from Dunhuang (5th to 10th centuries). Domestic scenes with oxen yoked to ploughs are seen in the wall-paintings of the life of the Buddha. Religious scenes are more common and it may be that these sketches of a monk on a dais (his patchwork robes making him look rather as if he has been tied up) and the fierce guardian figure below, were sketched by someone who worked on the great wall-paintings and banners.

8 Sutra.

The great *dhārani* of the Buddha mind. Apocryphal sutra, *Fo ding xin da tuo luo ni jing*, illustrated woodblock edition of the Ming (1369–1644).

[Or.80.d.21.]

In this small uncanonical Buddhist text, the page arrangement with its illustrations at the top recalls both the earlier 10th-century manuscript booklet of the Lotus sutra (5) and contemporary popular illustrated fiction (19). The format is one designed for popular editions, produced during the enormous expansion of printing under the Ming when bookshops were as 'thick as trees in a forest' in the commercial quarters of most cities. These small, cheaply produced booklets with pictures must have served a large audience with a fairly restricted vocabulary.

The illustration on the right depicts a butcher at work, committing one of Buddhism's cardinal sins, the taking of life which will be punished in hell. On the left, a pious couple read the sutras and burn incense; the text praises those who rise early for such religious devotions.

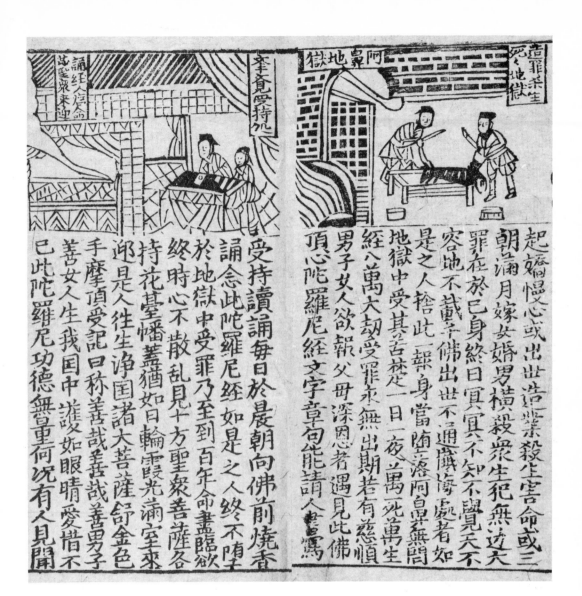

誦經人信來迎　　牽竟受持咒

起瞋愶心或出世造業殺生害命或三
朝潮月嫁女婚男橫殺衆生犯無边大
罪在於已身終日冥冥不知不覺天不
容地不戴予佛出世不遇﹍﹍海﹍者知
是之人捨此一報身當隨﹍落阿鼻無間
地獄中受其苦楚﹍一日一夜萬死萬生
經八萬大劫受罪無出期若有慈順
男子女人欲報父母深恩者遇見此佛
頂心陀羅尼經文字章句能請人書寫

受持讀誦每日於晨朝向佛前燒香
誦念此陀羅尼經如是之人命終不隨
於地獄中受罪乃至到百年命盡臨欲
終時心不散乱見十方聖衆善薩各
持花臺幡蓋猶如日輪霞光滿室來
迎是人往生淨国諸大菩薩舒金色
手摩頂受記曰称善哉善哉善男子
善女人生我国中﹍﹍如眼睛愛惜不
已此陀羅尼功德無量更何況有人見聞

9 The Qi sha tripitaka.
Woodblock edition with
frontispiece; one *juan* of
6,362. Jiangsu province, 1301.
[Or.80.d.25.]

One of the greatest printing
enterprises in China was the
first printing of the Buddhist
canon (or tripitaka), carried
out between AD 972 and 983
in Sichuan province. This
comprised 1,076 titles
translated from Sanskrit into
Chinese and printed in 5,048
juan (sections, sometimes
volumes). Four further
editions were printed during
the Song dynasty (960–1279).

In the mid-12th century,
the north of China was
invaded by a succession of
different rulers, mostly of
non-Chinese origin,
culminating in the Mongol
invasion which established
the Yuan dynasty in 1279.
This edition of the tripitaka
was begun in the southern
province of Jiangsu in 1231
but was not completed until
about 1322. The illustration
shows strong Tibetan
influence, for the Lamaist
Mongols were closely linked
to Lamaist Tibet.

The illustration is typical
of Buddhist printing. The
book itself is bound in the
concertina format, frequently
used for Chinese Buddhist
works which from the time of
the Diamond sutra onwards
often had lavish frontispieces
before the printed text.

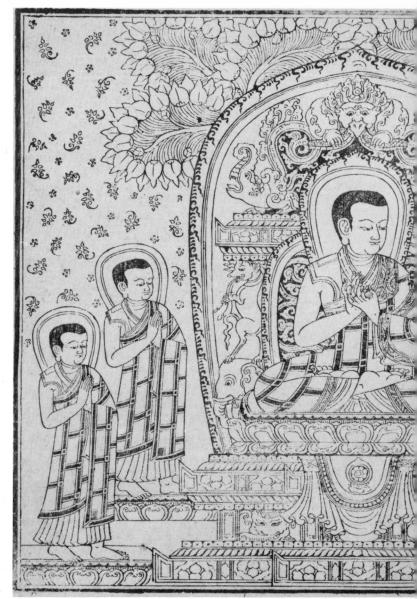

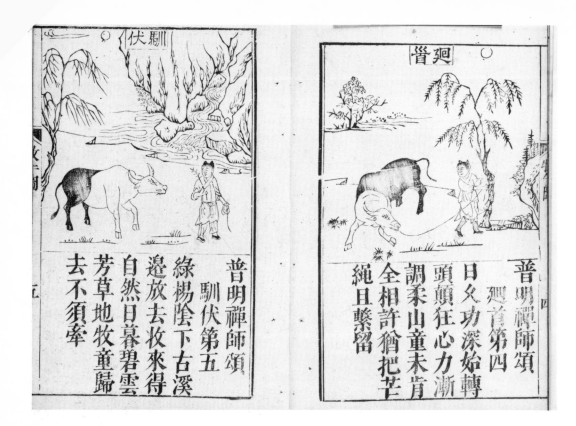

10 Tending the ox.

Mu niu tu, woodblock edition with half-page illustrations. Preface dated 1604.
[15101.c.28.]

A very popular *Chan* (Japanese: *Zen*) Buddhist text, the *Mu niu tu* seems to
have been published for the first time during the Song (960–1279) although its
association with previous *Chan* masters like Ma Zu, the 9th century patriarch,
suggest that it must have its origins in earlier teaching.

The ten illustrations depict a small herd-boy trying to 'tame' a water buffalo
but the allegorical significance relates to the idea of 'taming' one's own 'self'.
This is not done by force, but gradually, as can be seen in these two pictures,
fourth and fifth in the series. In the fourth, on the right, the herd-boy is
beginning to be able to control the animal; the picture is called 'turning the
head'. In the fifth, on the left, control is almost complete for, as the text below
explains, when the herd-boy and his buffalo return home, the buffalo no longer
needs to be led on a string but follows his small master. In this edition, as in
many others, the point of the story is emphasised by the colouring of the
buffalo which gradually changes from black to white. He is blacker on the right
and increasingly white on the left as the two of them progress towards the
'taming' of the animal.

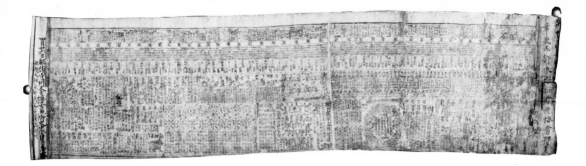

11 Calendar for the year 877.

Printed calendar found at Dunhuang; woodblock with diagrams.
[Or.8210/p.6.]

Though the private printing of calendars and almanacs was banned by imperial edict in 835, a number of examples found at Dunhuang indicate that quite a few printers took no notice of the ban. One fragment [Or.8210/p.10] even contains the information that it was printed in the Eastern Market of the capital Chang'an (modern Xi'an), under the noses of government officials.

This complete calendar and almanac, which is about four feet in length, does not bear a date but it contains internal evidence to date it to 877. It includes considerably more than just the days of the year; lucky and unlucky days are listed in detail and the twelve animals of the duodenary cycle are depicted (just left of the centre); below them (see detail, right) is a diagram of a typical courtyard house with all its elements in the correct position, to bring good luck.

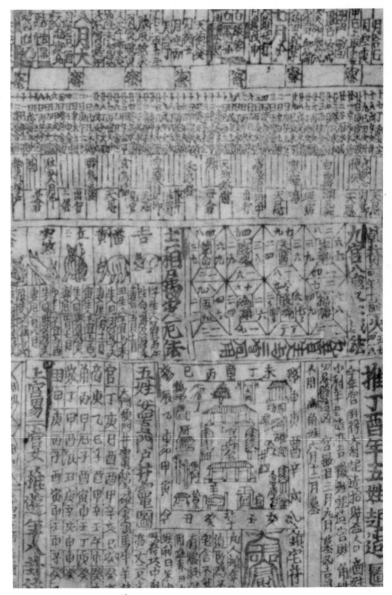

Traditional themes

Though the earliest surviving examples of printing are religious, secular printing grew fast enough to cause government concern as early as AD 835 when an edict prohibited the sale of block-printed unofficial calendars. During the Song (960–1279) the government continued to try to control printing by restricting certain categories – calendars, almanacs, examination cribs (especially miniature versions which could be smuggled into examination halls) and local descriptions which might be used for espionage. Attempts were made to force publishers to submit all works for government inspection before publication. Private publishers, too, attempted to curb unlicensed copying by claiming 'copyright' protection through government warrant; the first book with such a warrant was printed between 1190 and 1194.

It is clear from these (eventually unsuccessful) attempts at control that publishing was a huge industry catering for a growing audience, ranging from scholars with epigraphical and poetic interests to ordinary people who wanted to read romantic fiction and blood-and-thunder historical epics.

Illustrations were an integral part of many books, appearing in a variety of formats, from carefully produced and no doubt more expensive items with fine blockprints placed at intervals between the text, to the cheaper, cruder books with small illustrations at the top of every page. The latter format was common during the Ming; later Qing editions of popular fiction commonly contained a series of illustrations of characters or scenes grouped together at the beginning of the text.

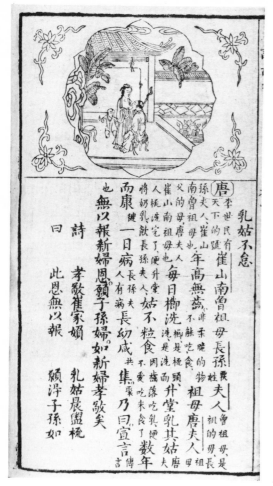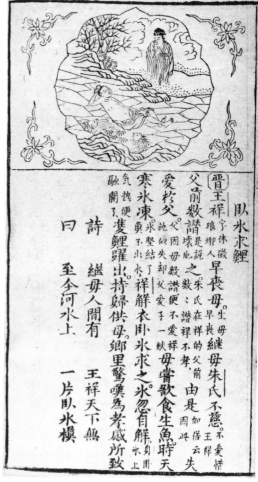

12 Twenty-four examples of filial piety.

Woodblock edition of the *Er shi si xiao* with illustrations in decorative cartouches. 1688.
[15319.b.20.]

The virtue of filial piety was upheld by Confucius and became an essential part of the ethos of family in traditional China. It was considered almost impossible for children to repay the bounty of their parents who had brought them into the world and cared for them.

On the right, a filial son removes most of his clothes to melt the ice on a frozen river so that his parents will have fresh fish to eat in winter. The text beneath records the 'historical' details of the exemplar, in this case a man called Wang Xiang. There follows a poem repeating the heroic deed.

On the left is a lady of the Tang dynasty (AD 618–907) suckling her elderly and toothless mother-in-law who could not take any other nourishment.

Even today, filial duties are taken seriously in China. Failing to care for elderly parents (without having to go to such lengths as here illustrated) is punishable by law and old people's homes only exist for those with no family at all.

13 Biographies of exemplary women.
Woodblock illustrated edition of the *Lie nü zhuan*, illustrations by Qiu Ying.
Preface dated 1779.
[15291.a.18.]

In traditional China, women were expected to have no independent life outside
the family, to obey first their parents, then their parents-in-law and husband
and finally, their sons. It was considered a disgrace for a woman to re-marry if
she was widowed; the most 'virtuous' thing she could do was to commit suicide.
Memorial arches commemorating virtuous widows who had killed themselves
were erected in almost every Chinese town.

It became the custom to append biographies of 'virtuous' women to the
dynastic histories where almost all the exemplars had sacrificed themselves in
one way or another to their husbands or husbands' families.

In this large collection devoted entirely to Confucian female virtue, the
women in the 24 examples of filial piety are included (one thoughtfully cutting
off a finger to feed an aged relative). Practically the only exception to these self-
destructive ladies is Mu Lan. Mu Lan was her parents' only child. When her
father was called up for military service, she disguised herself and went in his
place to avoid the disgrace that would fall on the family if nobody participated
in the war. She served for 12 years successfully concealing her sex and became a
folk heroine. She is depicted here in armour.

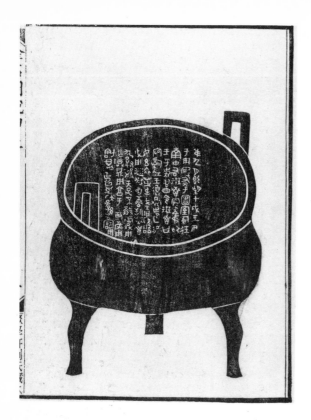

14 Illustrated work on bronze and stone.

Chu Jun's *Jin shi tu shuo* with commentaries by Niu
Yunzhen; preface dated 1745.
[15299.d.14.]

The study of ancient inscriptions began very early in
China and persists today. Some of the earliest
surviving writing appears in inscriptions on bones and
ritual bronzes of the Shang (*c*.1700–1066 BC) and Zhou
(1066–221 BC). The characters are the ancestors of
today's written forms but are in many cases almost
unrecognisable; indeed, their decipherment has
occupied scholars since the 1st century BC.

From that period, if not earlier, ink-squeezes (or
rubbings) were taken from stone inscriptions, and the
same technique was later used on bronzes to provide
collections of inscriptions for scholars and epigraphers.

In the *Jin shi tu shuo*, actual steles and bronze
vessels with inscriptions have been reproduced in
woodblock on a reduced scale by Chu Jun, a skilled
engraver who made a living from selling rubbings of
bronze and stone, in collaboration with Niu Yunzhen
(AD 1706–1758) a pedantic scholar, teacher and official.

On the left, an archaic bronze tripod is illustrated
with an inscription inside the vessel; on the right is a
copy of a stone stele bearing a small inscription and a
picture of the moon. The Chinese believed that a hare
lived in the moon, constantly pounding an elixir of
immortality with a pestle and mortar.

15 Views in the Garden of rarity.

Twenty-four woodblock illustrations of Wu Xinfu's
garden with accompanying poems. 1815.
[15323.b.15.]

Retired scholar-bureaucrats liked to construct gardens
where they could contemplate (man-made) nature, or
entertain friends with evenings of poetry-writing or
painting, accompanied by plenty of hot rice wine.

The construction of gardens was a literary and
philosophical pursuit, for they were considered
miniature versions of natural beauty, celebrated in
painting and poetry and revered by Taoist
philosophers. It was said that a Chinese gentleman was
'Confucian in office, Taoist in retirement and Buddhist
as death approached', summarising the eclecticism and
pragmatism of the Chinese religious view and giving a
context to the garden as a sort of Taoist retreat where
a man created his own mountain scenery without
having to climb.

At left, Wu Xinfu sits in an open-fronted hall,
supervising a servant boy (not visible) who is airing his
books in early summer. The accompanying poem
'Sunning books by the orchid steps' describes the
library in the 'Pavilion shaded by *tong* trees' amongst a
dozen pots of orchids in the west of the garden. In
southern China, where the climate is warm and damp,
books were stored in cedar or camphor boxes and aired
annually to prevent damp and insect damage.

In the illustration on the right one of the verandahs
of the house is depicted. It looks out over distant
mountains and a tranquil lake. This example of
Chinese garden design technique, where natural
features external to the tiny garden are made a focus,
is called 'borrowing a view'.

16 The romance of the lute.

Pi pa ji attributed to Cao Ming (born *c.* 1305). Woodblock edition with 41 illustrations by Huang Yibin and other members of the Huang clan. 1610. [Or.75.b.8.]

The drama *Pi pa ji* is thought to be one of the earliest examples of the southern drama, a combination of songs, dialogue and action usually with a romantic and uplifting plot. The plays were immensely long but relieved by songs, performed to a langorous accompaniment.

The story is a typical one. A young man worries about leaving his elderly parents when he goes off to take the exams for the imperial bureaucracy. His father insists that he go, and he comes first in the exam. An overnight celebrity, he is forced to marry the Prime Minister's daughter. Meanwhile his parents starve to death in a famine and his first wife sets off to tell him the news, supporting herself on her journey by playing the lute. The hero returns to mourn his parents for the traditional three years (together with both wives) and eventually, mourning over, returns to the capital to take up office. As both wives have been models of filial virtue, this is considered to be a happy and satisfactory ending.

The illustrations to this early edition are by famous block-cutters and the work is remarkably detailed, particularly in the fine line of the fabric and tile patterns. Here, the hero is being congratulated by the Prime Minister on his exam success and is about to receive his official hat.

17 The Disused kiln.
Illustrated edition of the *Po yao ji* by Wang Dexin of the Yuan (1279–1368). Published in Nanjing between 1573 and 1620.
[Or.81.d.2.]

The drama, half-sung, half-spoken, is typical. It tells the story of an impoverished scholar who falls in love with the beautiful daughter of a high official. They run away together but poverty forces them to live in a disused brick kiln (lovers in Chinese stories often hide in such places) and to beg for food. Whilst the scholar goes off to the capital to take higher exams, his lover is menaced by a tiger. The tiger leaves, the young man is offered a high government appointment and the play ends happily with her parents consenting to their marriage.

This copy is perhaps unique as this edition is not included in Chinese collections, though it is mentioned in the major reference works on Yuan drama. The text is surrounded by a 'gold-jade' border and there are 18 illustrations placed throughout the text. The size of the illustrations and the clarity of the text suggest that this might have been quite an expensive popular text.

18 The Dream of the Red Chamber.

Woodblock edition of 1811 published by the Tong guan ke and a modern metal type imprint of *c*. 1880. [15333.a.1. and 15326.d.5.]

Cao Xueqin's novel, one of the best-known pieces of Chinese fiction, was first published in 1792, some thirty years after his death. The story tells of the triangular love between the hero and two of his cousins (with various subsidiary flirtations) set amongst the doings of the large aristocratic Jia family.

The 1811 edition (left) has crude woodblock illustrations reminiscent of those found in Ming books. The illustration shows the Jia family ancestral hall with a rather daft-looking lion on a stone plinth outside. This is obviously intended to represent one of the stone or bronze lions to be seen outside major halls in, for example, the Forbidden City, and gives some idea of the grandeur of the Jia family mansion.

Cao Xueqin's grandfather entertained the Kangxi Emperor and his retinue on four of his six tours to the south, made between 1684 and 1707 (see also **28**). In order to receive the imperial visitor, a separate residence with gardens was built, an episode which Cao Xueqin fictionalised in chapters 16 and 17. The latter chapter, illustrated in the 1880 edition (right), describes how some of the gentlemen of the Jia family add the finishing touches to a traditional Chinese garden. Five men with archaic hairstyles (they should have the long pigtail, imposed by the Manchus in 1644) stand in a typical southern garden, trying to think of poetic names for pavilions, in order to add a literary and calligraphic finishing touch. For the Chinese, part of the fun of visiting a garden lay in trying to trace references in pavilion names and couplets carved on rocks. In this way, the garden became a sort of literary panel game as well as a pretty place.

The unvaried but fine line of the metal-type edition contrasts strongly with the angular strokes of the traditional woodblock and shows the speed of change in printing techniques during the 19th century.

19 The Romance of the Three Kingdoms.

San guo zhi zhuan, Yu Xiangwu's woodblock illustrated edition, Shuang feng tang, 1592.
[15333.e.1.]

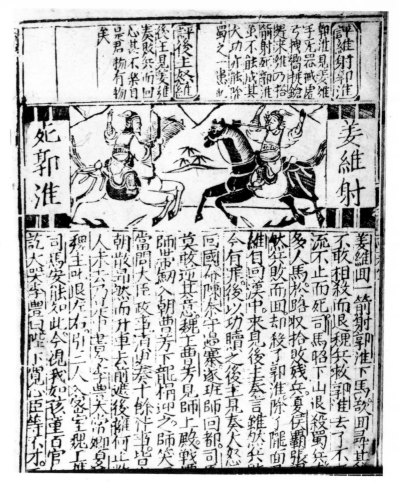

One of the most popular fictional genres in China was and still is the historical epic, a romanticised tale based on real events and characters. The Romance of the Three Kingdoms, first published in novel form by Luo Guanzhong (*c.* 1330–*c.* 1400), based on oral story-tellers' versions, is perhaps the earliest and best known example. It describes the period from AD 168 to 265 when the rulers of three kingdoms contested for absolute power. The main characters are Liu Bei, the legitimate Han heir, the wily Cao Cao of Wei and the vacillating Sun Quan of Wu. The most developed characters are their generals; Liu Bei's commander Zhuge Liang has passed into Chinese folklore as a supernatural military and technical genius.

Here Jiang Wei, an ambitious man of humble background who had attached himself to Zhuge Liang is shown being shot in the eye in battle (right). Though a distinguished soldier, he was eventually defeated by the Wei army.

The format is typical of late Ming popular editions, with an illustration heading each page; in this edition, the illustration and the text are clear and well-cut – which was not always the case in popular editions.

20 Journey to the west.

Xi xiang ji by Wu Cheng'en, woodblock edition with illustrations. 18th century.
[15271.c.13.]

The Journey to the West (partially translated by Arthur Waley as *Monkey*) is a 16th-century novel very loosely based on Xuan Zang's epic trip to India to collect the Buddhist sutras in the 7th century. As with other 'historical' novels, reality and magic are intertwined and inseparable.

Xuan Zang (*c.* 596–664), though not the first, was probably the most famous of all Buddhist pilgrims, travelling for 16 years, to return to the Chinese capital with 520 cases of Buddhist texts from India. He spent the rest of his life translating them. His journey involved considerable dangers and excitements, but in Wu Cheng'en's story the journey is transformed into an epic of supernatural events. As with the Romance of the Three Kingdoms, it seems likely that the story was based on earlier narratives.

One of the most puzzling aspects (for literary historians) is the nature of the two main companions of Xuan Zang (known in the novel as Tripiṭaka, after the Buddhist texts he was seeking). The most prominent is 'Monkey', a completely fabulous figure and in many ways the real hero of the book, for his fantastic cunning and supernatural gifts frequently save Tripiṭaka from demons, brigands and warriors. In contrast, the figure known as 'Pigsy' is earthy in the extreme, without a trace of magical power, unable to free himself from the human and animal desires that Buddhists sought to eliminate.

In Chapter 23 Pigsy falls into a trap. On the right, he is seen accepting food whilst Monkey and Tripiṭaka stand aloof. On the left, Pigsy is blindfolded in an attempt to decide which girl should marry him. The episode ends in disappointment, for the women and the food were illusory – sent as a test of adherence to Buddhist precepts, rather as St Anthony was tempted.

21 Record of the Western ocean.

Xi yang ji by Luo Maodeng. Woodblock edition with illustrations, published from worn blocks possibly from the 1597 edition.
[15331.f.2.]

Another historical romance or romanticised history, the *Record of the Western ocean* tells of the great sea voyages of the eunuch Zheng He between 1405 and 1433.

Zheng He, a moslem from Yunnan, served at court in the early Ming period, during which time he organised seven maritime expeditions to India, the Persian Gulf, East Africa and Mecca. The inspiration for the voyages is not certain; it may have been to try and expand China's spheres of influence, or it may have been trade, though nothing much came of them apart from a few curiosities brought back to the court.

The expeditions did however demonstrate the effectiveness of the newly perfected maritime compass (first regularly used at the beginning of the 12th century in China, some time before it was introduced into Europe by Arabs) and improved ship-building techniques.

The illustration shows how myth and fact are mixed in these novels. Although in the historical voyages normal ships were used, the boats depicted here are said to have been constructed with the help of the totally legendary master-builder and magical carpenter, Lu Ban. The patron saint of carpenters, Lu Ban was credited with building and technical miracles throughout China's history, solving problems that had baffled experts. Officials in black hats with flaps inspect these magically produced and somewhat unconvincing boats.

道大成盆鼓休子莊

劉元
普漢
子生
貴

22 Strange sights ancient and modern.

(19th century?) Woodblock print of *Xiu xiang jin gu qi guan*, 40 *juan* originally compiled by Bao wen lao ren (pseud.), 1632–1644.
[15331.e.12.]

In this collection of historical stories and myths, 20 illustrations in circular cartouches precede the text, a common form of arrangement in later popular woodblock editions. In this collection the illustrations are almost superfluous since the stories are so well-known.

The famous philosopher Zhuang zi (*c*. 3–4th century BC), whose ideas contributed to the development of the Taoist school, is shown at left beside a grave mound with its surrounding wall. It is told that he was found cheerfully drumming on a basin and singing after his wife died. He explained that though he had grieved at first he came to see her death as part of the cycle of life which echoes the cycle of the seasons; and now that she was sleeping peacefully in the Great Inner Room, he wasn't going to disturb her by struggling against a natural process.

23 Record of the Eight Immortals.

Illustrated woodblock edition of *Ba xian chu shen zhuan* by Wu Yuantai. Possibly 17th century.
[15334.e.6.]

The Eight Immortals are all legendary Taoist adepts who achieved immortality, for it was part of popular Taoist belief that physical immortality, achieved often through alchemy, ensured spiritual immortality. The later illustrated album (45) *A keepsake from the cloud gallery* contains illustrations of similar adepts, not as well-known individually as the eight, of whom three were historical personages the others totally mythical.

Lü Dongbin is depicted saving a sheep from a hungry tiger by interposing his body between the two, a prosaic act in an otherwise eventful life full of walking on the clouds of heaven, flying through the air, slaying dragons and ridding the earth of evils. Lü is one of the rare immortals to be based on a real person. He was born in 755 into a family of high officials. At the age of 20, he met a fire-dragon who presented him with a sword which magically enabled him to hide himself in the sky.

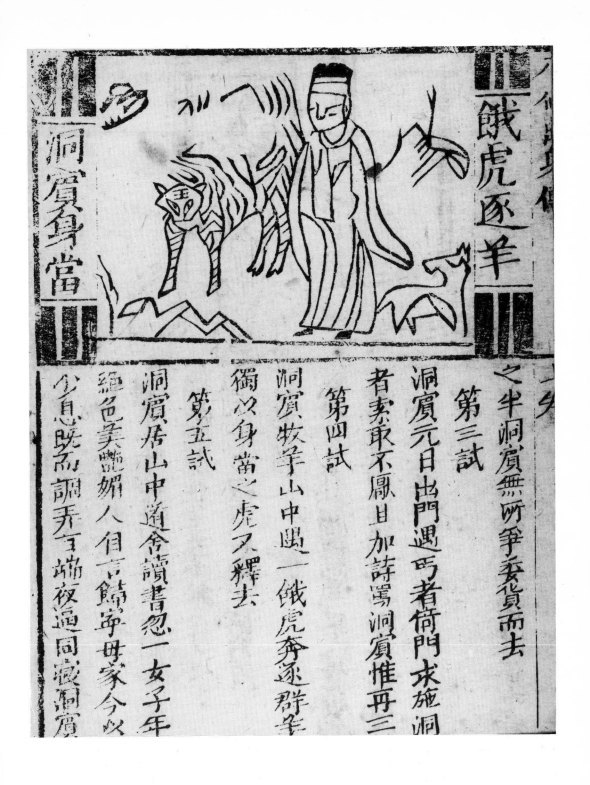

之半洞賓無所爭委貨而去

第三試

洞賓元日出門遇丐者倚門求施洞
者賣取不屑且加詩罵洞賓惟再三

第四試

洞賓牧羊山中遇一餓虎奔逐群羊
獨以身當之虎又釋去

第五試

洞賓居山中讀書忽一女子年
絕色美艷媚人自言歸寧母家今以
少息曉而調弄百端夜通同處洞賓

高詠樓
舊傳宋蘇軾
題西江月詞
於此居人建樓
以誌遺韻曰蜀
岡朝旭乾隆二
十七年
賜今名

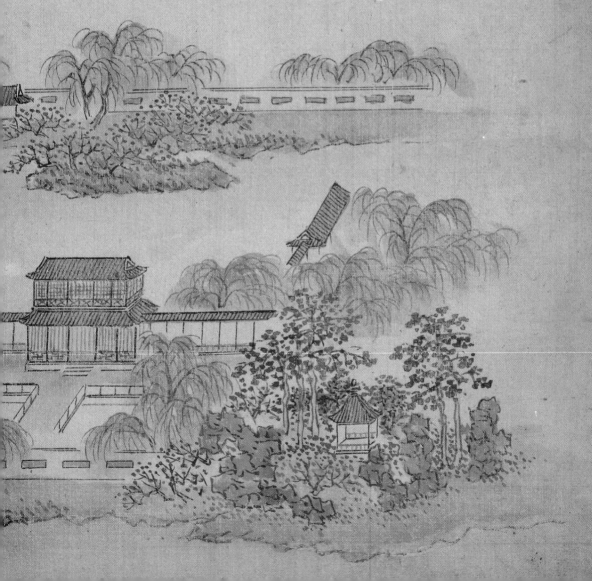

Some 'imperial' editions and related works have been included in other chapters in this book – such as works on technology and the lithograph of celebrations for the Kangxi emperor – and they give an indication of the wide variety of works produced in and for the court. Many works were published by the court, which from the Tang period had seen bibliography and preservation of the cultural heritage (and censorship) as part of its function. During the Qing, the court printers were particularly prolific and inventive, experimenting with movable type and copper engraving, as well as producing manuscripts to illustrate, for example, imperial journeys and events.

24 An Imperial encyclopaedia.
'Synthesis of books and illustrations of ancient and modern times', *Qin ding gu jin tu shi ji cheng*, in 32 sections, 10,000 volumes, printed with copper movable type, 1728.
[15023.b.1.]

Since the Southern Song (AD 1127–1279) the Chinese have published encyclopaedic works (or 'collectanea'), in which a variety of quite separate books, by different authors from different periods, are re-published together because they are linked in some way. The *Tu shu ji cheng* is slightly different in that it does not include whole works but groups quotations and extracts from earlier works by subject; it is therefore a type of classified dictionary of reference and quotation.

It was begun by Chen Menglei (born 1651), and finally printed in an edition of 64 in 1728. The font of copper type cast for the printing comprised over a quarter of a million pieces and was so valuable that shortly after use it was melted down for coinage. (Later grand imperial printing projects either reverted to traditional block-printing or used wooden type as both methods were infinitely cheaper.)

Some sections are illustrated with technical, explanatory drawings. The section on rabbits has an illustration which accompanies quotations from earlier works such as the *Er ya* (a lexicographical work of the 2nd century BC) which states that rabbits conceive by looking at the moon and another which says that they give birth through the mouth.

兔圖

25 The imperial summer resort.

Yu zhi bi shu shan zhuang. Han-i araha Alin-i tokso de halhun be jaiĺaha gi bithe [The Kangxi Emperor's poems describing the summer resort at Chengde], preface dated 1711, postface dated 1712, Chinese–Manchu. Illustrated copper-engraved edition by Matteo Ripa.
[19957.c.4.]

The Qing court spent a considerable portion of the summer months in a large palace about 150 kilometres north-west of Beijing, near the small town of Chengde which used to be called Rehe ('warm river') and was known to foreigners as Jehol. The first parts of the palace were built there by the Kangxi Emperor in 1703 and named *Bi shu shan zhuang* 'The mountain village where you can escape the heat'. 'Village' suggests a humble group of cottages, rather than the huge park with a surrounding wall 20 kilometres long containing a multitude of buildings, a vast library, dozens of garden pavilions and thousands of fruit trees.

The park, which still stands, wonderfully conveys the splendour of the early Qing and the confident grandeur of imperial China. The false humility of its name is characteristic of traditional *politesse* where one's own possessions and attributes are automatically denigrated and those of others automatically 'honourable'.

This handsomely illustrated volume contains illustrations of many of the buildings within the great enclosure. A lyric describing this water-side pavilion reads:

A mountain suddenly rises from the lake,
Flat-topped with a three-roofed pavilion.
To the north is the Hall of the supreme god,
above are layers of cloud,
below is azure water.

To ascend it is like climbing a magical peak;
The north is enclosed in banks of cloud,
to the open south, scenes merge into a view.

The poem is attributed to the Kangxi emperor, but,
as with his poems in the *Geng zhi tu* it is not certain
whether he actually composed it himself.

The verses are printed both in Chinese and Manchu
(the native language of the Qing ruling house) in
separate fascicules, but the Manchu versions do not
have the extensive notes appended to the poems in the
Chinese sections.

26 Ceremonial objects of the court.

2nd (Palace) edition of Jiang Pu's *Huang chao li qi tu
shi*, first published in 1759. This edition, woodblock
with illustrations, 18 sections, published in 1766.
[15300.e.1.]

Qing court costume was codified in 1759 by imperial
edict and the first publication of the *Huang chao li qi tu
shi* in the same year reinforced the idea of sumptuary
regulations and imperial design. The work, in 18
sizable sections, contains descriptions and illustrations
of far more than just court costume (as the illustrated
silk manuscripts like **27** might suggest) and also far
more court costumes than the restricted range copied
in colour. The outer coat worn by a 5th rank courtier
(see p.4), is illustrated here, together with one of the
Emperor's 6 rainhats.

The work also includes many sections illustrating
ritual vessels and implements used in worship,
astrolabes, time-pieces, chairs and tables, ritual
banners and standards. There is much detail in the last
few sections of military and hunting equipment,
including 63 different sorts of arrow for hunting
different animals, birds and fish as well as spears,
swords, cannon, banners and blunderbusses.

In this particular work the illustrations are
fundamentally technical. The fact that their decorative
potential was also obvious is demonstrated in the
copies made for export (see next page).

garment, too, which is not true of paintings.

Garments depicted include the *pu fu* or dark silk outer coat worn by a courtier of the fifth rank (see pages 4, 5). From 1759, sumptuary regulations required all (male) members of the court to wear *pu fu* with a square of silk tapestry or embroidery sewn on back and front denoting the rank of the wearer. In this case it is the silver pheasant, as opposed to the lesser egret of the sixth rank or the eighth rank quail.

The yellow silk gown with embroidered dragon medallions was for the Empress Dowager and the dark-blue dragon coat was a winter court robe for the sons of imperial princes.

The court costumes of China differed from those of ordinary people in quality but were otherwise similar to those of all but manual labourers, who wore short jackets and trousers. The narrow looms used affected the construction of clothing, necessitating a centre back seam and full front opening. The *pu fu* with its back seam and wide straight sleeves is in the Chinese tradition though the crossed-over front fastening is a Manchu innovation, based on the shape of animal hides and, by virtue of its double thickness, offering better protection from the wind for mounted nomads.

27 Export album of court costumes.

Manuscript paintings on silk based on the *Huang chao li qi tu* [Illustrations of ceremonial objects of the court, 1759, 1766]. 19th century? [Or.9430.]

These detailed and accurate silk paintings are exact reproductions of some of the court costumes described in the *Huang chao li qi tu* (see page 43). Just as in the original, the rank of the wearer is noted but the woodblock edition contains more explanatory text and often illustrates the back of a

28 The stations of Qianlong's 5th journey.

Album of paintings, ink and colour wash on silk; the last painting signed by Qian Weicheng (1720–1772). [Or.12895.]

The Qianlong Emperor (1711–1799) made six trips to the

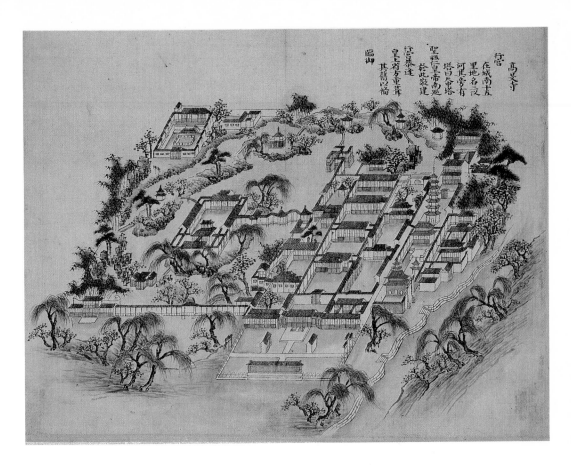

Yangtze area. Illustrated albums record the places where he stayed, some well-known beauty spots like the 'Tower of exalted Singing', some newly constructed garden-house complexes like that described in the *Dream of the Red Chamber* (18).

The illustration on pages 38 and 39 depicts a garden in spring, with the light pink of prunus blossom washed over the branches. The garden, surrounded by a white-washed wall with open-work windows lined with grey bricks, contains all the essentials of a Chinese garden – water, strangely-shaped rocks, pine, prunus and willow trees and pretty little pavilions set amongst them. The place is called the 'Tower of

exalted singing' and the colophon states that the famous poet Su Shi (1036–1101) wrote a poem there. Thus, the garden is further significant for its poetic connections.

The painter who signed the last painting in the album was also known as a calligrapher and is said to have modelled his calligraphic style on that of Su Shi who, apart from being a poet was known as a calligrapher and painter of bamboo.

The illustration above is one of the temples that the Emperor stayed in, the 'Autumn Sky Temple'. It is a more technical painting, clearly illustrating the plan of the temple with its side buildings reached by garden

walkways, the pagoda and the fanciful swastika-shaped pavilion (the swastika is a Buddhist emblem of good fortune).

The style of the painting is fairly unusual in that the albums do seek to record actual places associated with the Emperor's journeys. Thus although they employ many characteristic devices of traditional paintings, they are also reasonably faithful records of sites and buildings.

Later printing and export paintings

The 19th century saw great changes as China came face to face with the industrialised, expansionist west. The East India Company, from its base in Canton, exported porcelain, tea, silks, furniture, wallpaper and other decorative items including paintings made especially for the European market.

It is ironic that the country which invented printing and which had abandoned experiments with movable type as being too cumbersome because of the nature of the Chinese language and script, should be introduced to lithographic processes and, eventually, movable type, by Europeans in the 19th century.

Despite the introduction of new printing processes, traditional methods continued to flourish. The coloured 'New Year' prints, which at first reproduced traditional figures such as protective door-gods, and later depicted operatic scenes and even recent political events, were printed in a great number of regions, and are still produced in Tianjin, Shanxi and Shandong. The craft of fine colour printing was revived in the 1930s to continue in Beijing, where it can still be seen.

29 One-man puppet show.

Export album of paintings representing trades and occupations, 19th century.
[Or.2262.]

In contrast with traditional Chinese painting, export albums are highly coloured and painted in a more solid 'Western' style. Here, a grandfather has taken his grandchild to watch a street puppet show, where the single operator also supports the stage on his shoulders. The puppet drama may well be a familiar scene from a traditional opera, since it apparently involves an official in a black ear-flapped cap, perhaps a judge presiding over a court (quite a familiar operatic theme). Contemporary accounts record the enormous number of entertainers on Chinese streets. They can still be seen today, juggling or performing acrobatics, sometimes with a monkey to collect money from passers-by.

30 Street scenes.

Sweet and toy-seller and an old man taking his birds out for a walk. Export album of street scenes and occupations, ink and colour wash on paper; 19th century.
[Or.11539.]

The streets of traditional Chinese cities would be thronged with water-sellers, street performers, peddlars and menders of all sorts, many of whom had special street-cries or banged drums or gongs to announce their arrival. One of the favourite street-tradesmen was the toy or sweet-seller and they can still be seen in China, making flat silhouettes of fish, chickens, dragons or cats out of dark-brown toffee or twisting small coloured strips of dough to form dolls. The street-trader shown above right has a small gong and sells his wares from a painted box whose form is reminiscent of the old Chinese silver ingot. He sells a variety of goods, including small toy figures. The clothing of the child with his brocade waistcoat over a long gown contrasts with the more practical short gown of the salesman.

The bird-fancier (right) must also be a gentleman of some means since he, too, wears a long gown with a shorter jacket over it (and not the short jacket and trousers of the peasant or poorer city-dweller). He carries two bird-cages, one covered in blue cloth, the other revealing the song-bird inside with his tiny red porcelain feeding bowls attached to the bamboo bars of the cage. Many Chinese today keep song-birds. It seems to be very much a man's hobby. The bird markets are always full of enthusiasts and outside

many houses in the cities one can see bird-cages hung out in the sun. Many people take their birds out for walks like this 19th-century gentleman; some even take them for bicycle rides.

31 Interior Scene.

Export album illustrating the evils of opium; colour on pith paper; 19th century.

[Or.7408.]

This is one of the less depressing scenes in the album, showing an interior with a group of musicians, mainly female. Their tiny bound feet can be seen peeping out from the trousers of the women on the far left and centre whilst the standing women appear to be wearing the high-platformed Manchu shoes. Since Manchu women did not bind their feet, these high shoes made the feet appear smaller than they were (a feature considered beautiful) without binding to force the toes underneath the instep. The women all wear three-quarter length coats over skirts or trousers – standard female clothing during the Qing (1644–1911). The one man playing a drum has the long plait worn by all men during the Qing, with the front part of his head shaved. Behind the orchestra is a couch-bed of carved wood with silk curtains and cushions and in the centre lies the equipment for opium smoking, including the pipe.

It is ironic that opium-smoking should have been a subject of fascinated horror for Europeans since it was Europeans who encouraged the habit in China, in order to foster the extremely lucrative business of selling Indian-grown opium there. The growth of dependence was such that the Chinese economy was seriously threatened and when the Chinese opium commissioner burnt a consignment of opium in Canton, China found itself at war with Britain (1839–40).

32 Silkworms spinning cocoons.

Chinese export painting on paper, 19th century.
[IOLR NHD 43.]

Export paintings were part of the cargoes sent back to Europe by the ships of the East India Company in the late 18th and 19th centuries. Trades and occupations or handicrafts were commonly depicted. Quite a number of series were produced, showing the process of manufacture of tea, ceramics or silk, and this illustration is one of a series depicting not so much the manufacture of silk as the process by which the silkworms grow and spin their cocoons. In the first pictures in the series, the worms are tiny specks on great mulberry leaves but they grow enormous and fat and here are seen in a late stage of transformation, spinning cocoons on a specially constructed lattice. Such detailed technical paintings are not at all typical of Chinese art but were made to appeal to the European taste for botanical and zoological paintings.

33 River transport in southern China.

Chinese export painting on paper. 19th century.
[IOLR Add. Or. 1967/61.]

Travellers have long been fascinated by the water-transport and the water landscape of China. They have always longed to travel through the Yangtse gorges which, though not as dangerous as they were in the 19th century, still offer scenes of small boats being hauled upstream by trackers (never now as far or as hard as in the past as modern powered boats have taken over the heavy, long-distance work), the occasional junk with its square patched sail with bamboo ribs (like the distant junk in this painting), and fantastic scenery.

The painting depicts southern China, showing the paddy-fields with their narrow raised paths and a variety of river transport. The small boat being hauled upstream is the sort of boat that commonly was home for the river workers of China (and is still used as such in some of the southern regions where people live from fishing or short haulage – cooking, eating, sleeping, washing and working on board).

34 Chinese furniture from the East India Company.
Chinese export painting of bamboo furniture made for the East India Company. Colours on paper, 19th century.
[IOLR Add. Or. 2331.]

From the outset, the object of the East India Company was two-way trade with the East. Earlier, when Chinese porcelain was tremendously in demand in Europe (in the 17th and 18th centuries), the EIC organised 'made-to-order' services in which goods could be ordered in London, them made and decorated in China and shipped back to Europe, packed in china clay in the ship's hold (helping as ballast and protection for the more delicate cargoes of tea and silks). The EIC had sample plates, with different rim patterns and decorations from which their clients to choose; some of these can still be found in the collections of the Victoria and Albert Museum in London.

Similarly, pattern books illustrating other articles for shipment were made in China for the Company. In an album consisting mainly of more ornate pieces of furniture, this smaller, simpler bamboo chair appears – looking exactly the same as the bamboo chairs that are used all over southern China today.

35 Panorama of Peking.

The celebrations of the Kang xi Emperor's 60 years on the throne. Photolithographic edition based on an earlier illustrated woodblock edition, Shanghai, Dian shi zhai, 1879.

[15297.a.15.]

The Chinese consider a sixtieth birthday an occasion for great celebration, and many gifts are presented – often symbols of longevity like peaches.

The Kang xi Emperor (Kang xi, meaning 'vigorous and splendid' was a reign-name, not a personal name) celebrated his 60th year on the throne in 1721. Such grand celebrations, which included triumphal processions through the streets of the capital, were usually commemorated by hand-scroll manuscript illustrations followed by cheaper, mass-produced printed versions, of which this is one. At the top is a grand residence, its galleries hung with lanterns in celebration and with a raised stage in the centre for operatic performances. Below is an ordinary city street lined with shops, typical of late traditional architecture

in northern China, single-storeyed with grey roof-tiles and a raised roof-ridge. The long poles at the front of the shops were used to hang banners advertising the goods for sale. Behind the open-fronted shop building there would often be the enclosed courtyard of a private house with trees growing in the central open courtyard (left, centre and bottom). All manner of forms of transport can be seen, from horses to carts of more or less luxurious sorts, Chinese wheelbarrows (with the wheel under the load, not right at the front) and the shoulder-pole. There is even a man (left) scooping up the horse dung for manure.

There are virtually no women to be seen on the street for it was traditionally improper for women to venture out; even servant women tended to stay within the home. Women can be seen riding in covered carts (far right) and more elaborate horse-drawn carts (far left).

The illustration, although not finely drawn, is a very accurate picture of the streets of the capital city.

36 The celebration of Li Hongzhang's 70th birthday.

He fei xiang guo qi shi ci shou tu, photolithographic edition, Tianjin, 1892.
[15305.b.15.]

Li Hongzhang (1823–1901) was one of China's first outward-looking diplomats, challenging the Confucian tradition of self-sufficiency. He worked with 'Chinese Gordon' against the Taiping rebels (some of their letters are in the British Library's Chinese collection, donated by the Gordon family). A negotiator in many of China's rather unsuccessful foreign treaty discussions, he made a trip around the world, meeting Queen Victoria and the American President Cleveland in 1896.

The illustration is one of several from a celebratory album recording the events of his 70th birthday. Li's success as one of China's first 'ambassadors' is evident since the ambassadors of different nations are shown seated beneath their flags at a banquet with entertainers on stage (left). The large Chinese characters hung about the hall mean 'longevity'. The hall has been decorated with *pen cai* (better known in the West under their derived Japanese name of *bonsai*) and other pot-plants on stands.

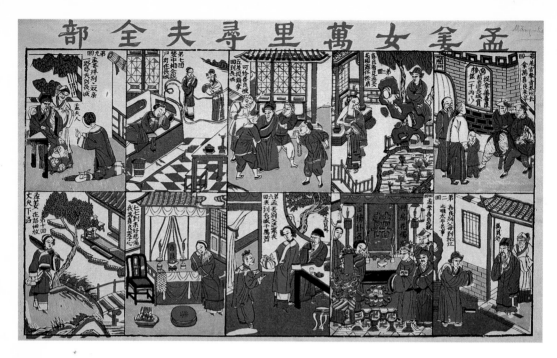

37 New Year print.

The story of the woman whose tears made the Great Wall fall down. One of a series of coloured woodblock 'New Year prints', early 20th century.
[Or. 5896.]

Meng Qiang nü is a well-known heroine of folklore. Her husband was sent off to build the Great Wall during the Qin (221–206 BC). He was gone for so long that her family threatened to marry her again to someone else, so she set off to look for him. When she reached the Great Wall, she was told that he had died; her tears made the wall fall down.

In this comic-strip version, the tale begins in the top right-hand corner and reads from right to left, ending in the bottom left-hand corner. The first picture announces that Wan Xiliang has been called up to work on the Great Wall; below, he bids goodbye to his parents, then (next column, top) he sees a girl in a garden and (below) he marries her, before being seized and sent off to the Wall. In the next column (top) Meng Qiang dreams that they meet again and speak at the Great Wall, whose battlements can be seen above the figures. The convention for illustrating events in a dream in Chinese books was to surround the subject of a dream with a sort of balloon, very like that used to enclose direct speech in a European cartoon strip. Finally Meng Qiang sets off in search of her husband. The rest of the sad tale is told on another poster.

'New Year prints' were so called because many of them were specially made for the Chinese New Year when they would be pasted up, both to decorate the house and to protect its inhabitants and bring them prosperity. This practice goes back to the Southern Song (1127–1279), if not earlier.

38 Accompanying the Empress.
Woodblock 'New Year' print in 6 colours. Shanghai, late 19th–early 20th century.
[Or.5896.]

Chinese opera, often called Peking opera in the West (a misleading term since every area in China has its own local form of opera) contains elements which have a very long history, though the genre as depicted in popular prints only dates back to the 18th century. The mixture of spoken monologues, songs, acrobatic fights and highly stylised gestures performed by actors in richly embroidered costumes was immensely popular in late traditional China and is enjoying a revival now, after being banned during the Cultural Revolution (1966–1976).

Many operas depicted well-known scenes from Chinese history, scenes which had also been incorporated into one of the favourite Chinese literary genres, the historical romance. This is a scene from an opera based on the history of the Three Kingdoms period (see **19**) where two of Liu Bei's generals (Guan Yu, centre with a red face and Zhang Fei, behind the city gate) were escorting two of Liu Bei's wives (left) when they were captured by Cao Cao. As the prisoners travelled to the capital, Cao Cao is supposed to have tested Guan Yu's loyalty and self-control by allotting only one room in which male and female prisoners were to sleep. Guan Yu stood up all night outside the room.

Operatic conventions are graphically depicted – for example, the mask-like face painting with its colour symbolism (green meaning fierceness; black, straightforwardness; red, loyalty), and the flat scenery of the city gate, with Zhang Fei perched on a table so that he can still be seen.

39 The Russian Army in difficulties.

'New Year' woodblock print in 5 colours, late 19th or early 20th century.
[Or.5896.]

Political subjects, particularly nationalistic events such as victories achieved in the Sino–Japanese war of 1894–5, were also depicted on the poster-size popular 'New Year' prints. Printed from 5 separate woodblocks in a crude, unpolished version of the more carefully executed technique of the late Ming colour prints, these were sold in single sheets to be pasted up on walls as decorations.

The lines of explanation alongside the title describe an incident at Shanhaiguan (where the Great Wall reaches the sea, on the border of Hebei and Liaoning provinces). Four Russian Navy vessels were sunk after a bombardment by the Chinese. Though the illustration is self-explanatory there are small captions here and there – 'Russian soldiers thrown into the sea', 'the head of a Russian soldier' and 'captured Russian soldiers.'

Sino–Russian relations were tense for much of the nineteenth and early 20th centuries and some of the border problems in dispute at that time are still points of contention.

40 Souvenir of the Guomindang's Northern Expedition.

Photolithographic poster in the style of the earlier woodblock 'New Year' prints. Shanghai, *c.* 1927.
[Or.5896.]

A more modern version of the 'New Year' print, using western printing technology in place of woodblocks, depicts the late Sun Yat-sen (1866–1925), first Director of the Guomindang (National People's Party) and, briefly, first President of the Republic of China (1911–1912). He is shown between nationalist flags and the characters in the frame around his head say 'The revolution is not yet completed; your comrades must continue to make efforts'. Below, his successor as leader of the Guomindang, Chiang Kai-shek, looking clean and youthful, waves a sword at his assembled troops who are about to try and continue the Northern expedition, during which they had already 'ferociously taken Changsha' (top left) and 'attacked and seized Yuezhou'.

The Northern expedition (1926–28) was an attempt to unify China, which had been split amongst various 'warlords' in charge of regional armies after Sun Yat-sen's failure to set up a strong central government. The Northern expedition was only partially successful; warlords continued to rule parts of China until 1949.

This poster is transitional in many ways; it marks the early use of western printing technology in China and in format stands between the popular woodblock 'New Year' print and the political poster which came to dominate in modern China.

奉天省俄軍受困圖

國民革命軍北伐記

41 Decorated letter-paper.

From the Ten Bamboo Studio. *Shi zhu zhai jian pu,* facsimile of the 1934 edition, Beijing, Rong bao zhai, 1952.

[Or.80.d.9.]

Together with the Ten Bamboo Studio Painting and Calligraphy handbook (**43**), Hu Zhengyan published a collection of decorated letter and poetry paper in the mid-17th century. Like the painting and calligraphy book, these separate sheets were colour-printed, using multiple woodblocks. Because the sheets were made for writing on, the area of decoration was more restricted than in the painting handbook and greater use was made of subtle intaglio printing where the paper was pressed onto carved blocks so that the design appeared in light relief. Though the size of the designs was necessarily restricted, in type they were very similar to those of the painting handbook, with birds, animals, still life and plants dominant.

The illustrations here depict scholarly figures, of the sort who would actually write poems or letters on this decorated paper, standing by a pine tree 'listening to the water', or lying against a rock reading (see page 6), or setting out with a small servant boy 'to visit the chrysanthemums'. These activities are typical of the refined scholarly gentleman and the figures are depicted in the same style as those in paintings.

Although the earliest surviving colour woodblock letter papers are mid-17th century, the tradition was revived in the 1930s by the noted bibliophile Zheng Zhenduo and the most prominent writer of the period, Lu Xun. Both were very interested in China's literary traditions and the history of printing in China. The art of colour woodblock printing and the production of decorated letter-paper had flourished in Beijing but was almost dead by the 1930s. Thanks to their encouragement, the craft was revived and continues today in the Rong bao zhai (Precious and Glorious Studio).

42 Chrysanthemum and wine.

One of 24 lithographs in a folding album, Beijing, Rong bao zhai, 1952.
[Or.74.d.2.]

The painter Qi Baishi (1863–1957) is one of the best known painters of modern China. Born into a very poor family, he had only one year of schooling and was apprenticed to a carpenter when young. Because of his skill, he soon began to carve complex decorative panels for furniture, and, in search of inspiration, looked at a copy of the *Mustard seed garden painting manual* (see **44**) from which he copied the illustrations. Thus in the time-honoured Chinese way – beginning by copying and mastering the elements and styles of previous masters – he taught himself to paint. He wrote the poems that accompany his paintings and also spent much of his time carving seals and practising calligraphy. Even in this lithograph, which contains only a signature and the words 'chrysanthemum' and 'wine', it is clear that the calligraphy and seal, placed within the design, are very much an essential part of the whole. In this, as in his use of strong colour, Qi Baishi, though not exactly an innovator, certainly developed elements of traditional painting into a personal and more 'modern' style.

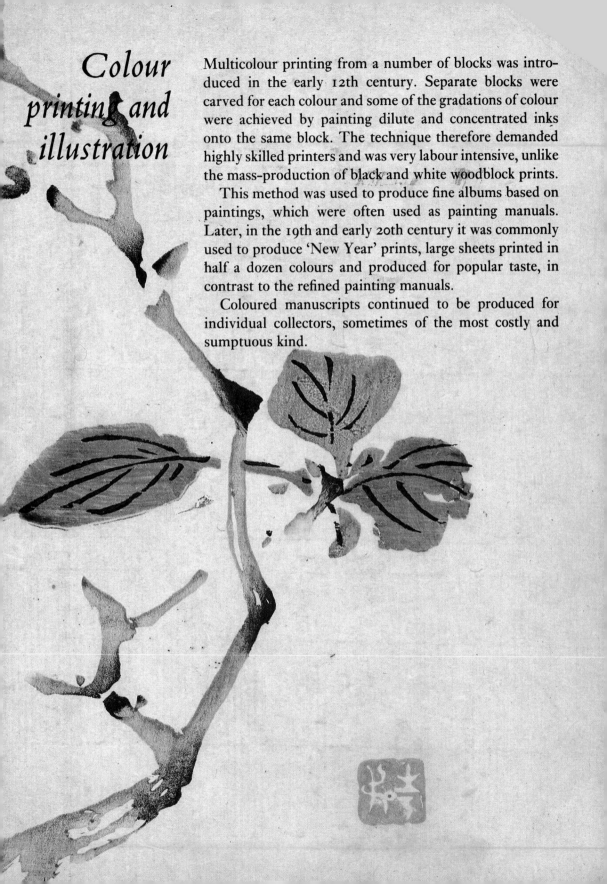

Colour printing and illustration

Multicolour printing from a number of blocks was introduced in the early 12th century. Separate blocks were carved for each colour and some of the gradations of colour were achieved by painting dilute and concentrated inks onto the same block. The technique therefore demanded highly skilled printers and was very labour intensive, unlike the mass-production of black and white woodblock prints.

This method was used to produce fine albums based on paintings, which were often used as painting manuals. Later, in the 19th and early 20th century it was commonly used to produce 'New Year' prints, large sheets printed in half a dozen colours and produced for popular taste, in contrast to the refined painting manuals.

Coloured manuscripts continued to be produced for individual collectors, sometimes of the most costly and sumptuous kind.

43 Colour prints from the Ten Bamboo Studio.

Shi zhu zhai shu hua pu, coloured woodblock albums,
c. 1643.
[Or. 59.a.10.]

The Ten Bamboo studio was the name of a house in
Nanjing where the scholar-painter friends of Hu
Zhengyan gathered. Hu Zhengyan was a fine amateur
calligrapher, painter and carver of seals. In the early
17th century he printed the collection of colour prints
from the Ten Bamboo Studio, which came to be the
best known of the early colour printed woodblock
books as well as the first painting manual to be printed
in colour.

The album contains colour prints classified by
subject: birds, fruit, prunus, orchids, bamboos, stones.
Each subject is treated in a variety of painterly styles,
some with hard outline and detail – as in the bird print
(see back cover illustration) where each feather is
carefully outlined – others, such as the picture of
lychees, treated in a lighter manner, as if painted with
a softer, wetter brush.

The albums from the Ten Bamboo Studio were so
popular that they were reprinted many times, often
from newly-cut blocks and not always with the same
attention to colour gradation and perfect matching of
blocks.

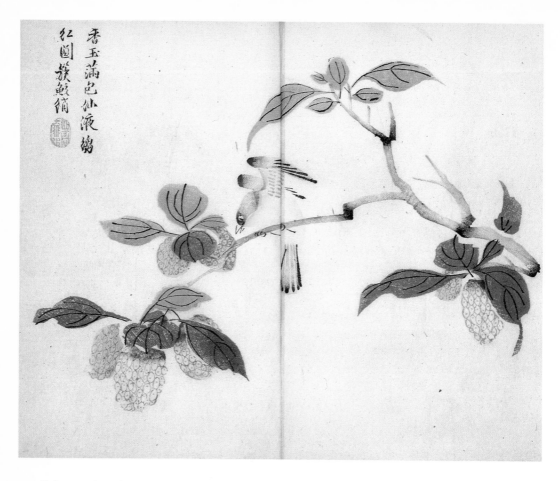

44 Colour prints from the Mustard seed garden painting manual.

Jie zi yuan hua juan, c. 1679–1701.
[15274.a.1.]

The Mustard seed garden painting manual was first
published in 1679 in Nanjing by the artist Wang Gai,
with two later sequels (1701) and thereafter in many
editions. Though similar to the Ten Bamboo Studio
albums (43) in intent, it is far more didactic – more
truly a painting manual for copying – than the Ten
Bamboo Studio prints. This is evident since the first
part of the first volume is an introduction to the
fundamental principles of Chinese painting and
subsequent sections break down the elements of a
landscape painting so that figures, boats, trees and
rocks can be separately copied and mastered before the
apprentice painter attempts his own composition from
these elements. Landscape compositions (not included
in the Ten Bamboo Albums) also appear, as in the
scene showing a fisherman in his boat beside an over -
hanging cliff, illustrated overleaf. The same variety of
techniques is shown; on the one hand, the soft line and
colour with which flowers, the bird and the lychees are
depicted, to be contrasted with the almost
monochrome design of the moon and bamboo, in
which the bamboo is depicted in single pressed-brush
strokes. There is far more use of calligraphy and seals
than in the Ten Bamboo Studio albums, making the
compositions more like 'real' paintings.

The technique of production is the same as that of
the Ten Bamboo Studio album.

67

45 (*facing page*)   A keepsake from the cloud gallery.

Large manuscript folio of *Yun tai xian rui* in
concertina form containing illustrations with
accompanying text; ink and colour on paper, 1750.
[Add.22689.]

This handsome folio must have been highly prized for
not only are the illustrations very finely painted but
the brocade binding and the case (*tao*) in which it was
kept are also beautifully made. It contains fifteen
paintings, each with an accompanying text describing
the miraculous behaviour of a Taoist adept.

The illustration here shows a man called Mei Fu
who served as an officer in the city of Nanchang. A
believer in Taoism, he wandered far in southern China
in search of immortals. He met a sage who taught him

alchemy; he went off into the Jilong (Chicken coop)
mountains but he failed in his alchemical experiments.
His teacher then descended from the clouds and told
him that his destiny was in Feihong (Flying swan)
mountain, and there he succeeded in achieving
immortality. One spring day, a group of immortal
ladies descended through the purple mists and clouds.
He greeted them, said farewell to his home and flew
off on a green phoenix.

The exquisitely detailed style of painting and the
lavish use of bright colour (together with the rather
fantastic subject-matter) stand in great contrast to the
academic restraint of the Ten Bamboo Studio or the
Mustard seed garden manuals and letter-paper.

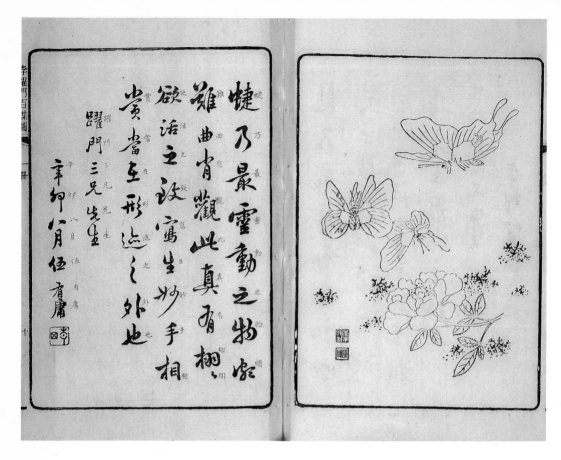

46 The hundred butterfly pictures.
Li Guolong's *Li Yuemen bai die tu*, illustrated with red
overprinting. Guangzhon, Xiao wen tang, 1849.
[15257.d.32.]

The album of illustrations of butterflies with
accompanying poems has been conceived very much as
a painting and calligraphy manual. The butterfly
illustrations have painters' seals carved in the
woodblocks (the top seal bears Li Guolong's name),
like proper paintings. The calligraphy and red
overprinting are didactic in purpose, for the running
style of the characters which makes them slightly
difficult to read is corrected by the small red 'standard'
character forms printed alongside. Thus even someone
who had some difficulty in recognising characters
written stylishly, could emulate the calligraphy and
actually know what he was writing.

The poem tells of the difficulty of capturing such
lively creatures with the brush.

Technical illustrations

Not all illustrated works were fictional. Woodblock illustrations also accompanied all sorts of technical works – from military manuals to guide-books and descriptions of traditional technology.

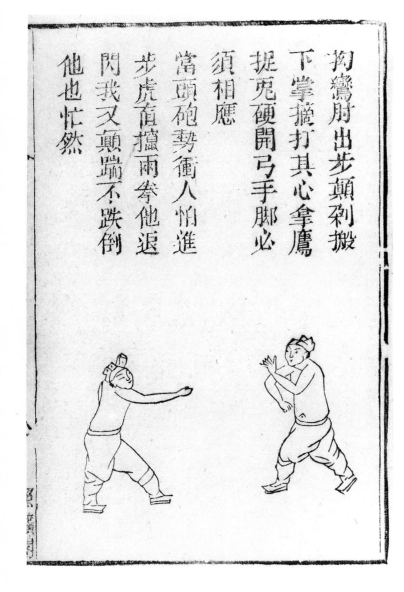

釣鸞肘出步顛剁搬
下掌摑打其心拿鷹
捉兔硬開弓手腳必
須相應
當頭砲勢衝人怕進
步虎直攛兩拳他退
閃我又顛踹不跌倒
他也忙然

47 A new treatise on tactics.
Woodblock print of Qi Jiguang's *Ji xiao xin shu* (1506), 1804.
[1525g.c.10]

Qi Jiguang (1528–1588) was one of the major military strategists of late Ming and early Qing China. For many years he was responsible for the maintenance of the southern coastal defences. Despite his status in the military, he is said to have been hen-pecked by his wife who is supposed successfully to have taken command of a fort surrounded by pirates.

This is a later edition of one of Qi's several books on tactics. He believed very strongly in the training of troops, a somewhat unusual attitude at that time for the Chinese traditionally viewed all soldiers as little better than bandits and used to say that good iron should not be made into nails and good sons should not go into the army.

The illustration depicts soldiers drilling in the martial arts, which Qi recommended as part of a soldier's training.

48 'A medical work on edibles'.

Zeng bu tu xiang shi wu ben cao hui zuan (Illustrated and expanded work on edibles and herbs) by Shen Lilong; woodcut with illustrations. 1691.

[15251.c.4.]

The compilation of *ben cao* (herbals or pharmacopoeia) has a long history in China, part of its equally long tradition of medical theory and treatment, which laid great stress on herbal remedies as well as the better-known acupuncture.

The earliest printing of a herbal was in 1108 and the best known and most important pharmacopoeia was compiled by Li Shizhen (1518–1593) who based his large work on previous herbals. His *Ben cao gang mu* (Detailed pharmacopoeia) included minerals, animal and botanical sections which appear in all later compilations, of which this is one. Chinese herbals, which were frequently illustrated as a guide to identification, are thus a mixture of pharmacopoeia and natural history – though it should be remembered that, as in European traditional medicine, parts of animals were used in medicines.

The illustration from this herbal (which is only slightly later than Li Shizhen's *Ben cao gang mu*) depicts in the top row (left to right) a gorilla, ape, and hedgehog, and below a baboon, a sort of long-tailed monkey and an unvariegated small monkey holding a peach.

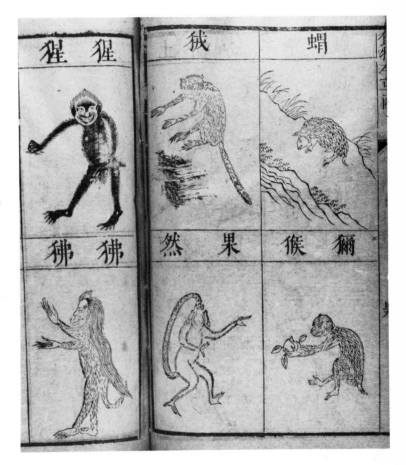

49 The creations of nature and man.

The *Tian gong kai wu* of Song Yingxing. Woodblock print with illustrations. Facsimile of a print of 1637.
[15226.b.19.]

Towards the end of the Ming dynasty (1368–1644) there was a growth of interest in technical matters which was to continue into the Qing. It may be argued that, as China found itself unprepared for the technological West in the mid-19th century, this interest was not very effective or deeply explored but it nevertheless represented an attempt to break free from the traditional divisions between the intellectual and the manual. Song Yingxing, the author, himself suggests in his preface that this work was not likely to advance his official career much, since technology was not part of the imperial civil servant's concern.

Song Yingxing was a native of Jiangxi province and most of the activities depicted in the work, which include mining (of coal and copper), rice production, silk weaving and ceramic production, were practised in the province and so were probably very familiar to him.

Each section is fully illustrated; the illustration here is taken from the ceramic section. Porcelain produced at Jingdezhen in Jiangxi was one of the most sought-after products in the world. At the period in which Song was writing porcelains were about to be imported into Europe in considerable quantities for the first time. Blue and white porcelains (decorated with cobalt under the glaze) still dominated production in Jingdezhen, although a new fashion for enamelled wares in a greater variety of colours was beginning. The illustrations show potters decorating the wares (left). The man in the foreground is painting in cobalt onto the body of the ware, while beyond him sits a man at a wheel who is painting fine blue lines around the rim of a small bowl. On the right, two men are dipping the painted ware into a great bowl of glaze prior to firing. The same process can still be seen in Jingdezhen which continues to produce much of China's porcelain.

瓷汶器水

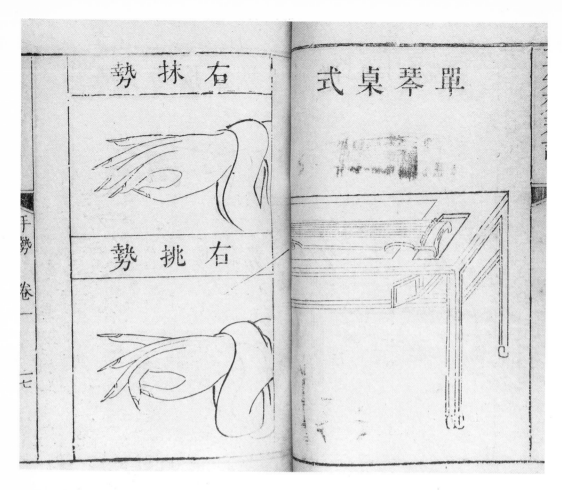

50 Music book for the *qin*.
From the study of the five diligences. Woodblock print with illustrations,
Wu zhi zhai qin pu by Zhou Zi'an, 1746.
[15257.e.7.]

Apart from being able to write poetry in a fine hand, remember lengthy
passages of classical literature and paint a passable picture, the traditional
Confucian gentleman was also supposed to appreciate music. There are a
number of illustrated music primers and this one, with its technical illustrations
of hand positions, teaches how to play the *qin*, a seven-stringed instrument that
was placed on top of a table (right). It was obviously necessary to grow long
fingernails to enable one to pluck the strings.

51 Tilling and weaving.
From an Imperial picture
album. *Yu zhi geng zhi tu*,
illustrated by Jiao Bingzhen
with poems attributed to the
Kangxi emperor, (1696).
Edition of *c.* 1750.
[15268.b.7.]

The original *Geng zhi tu* was
produced by Lou Shou
(1090) and published in about
1237. It contained
illustrations depicting the
cultivation of rice and the
process of sericulture and silk
weaving, as does this later
imperial reprint.

The seven character poems
above the illustrations in this
later version are apparently in
the emperor's hand
(reproduced in woodblock)
though it is not possible to be
certain whether he actually
wrote the poems or
'borrowed' them from
scholars at the court.

The illustration depicts silk
reeling. After the silk cocoons
form, they are plunged into
boiling water (which
naturally kills the silkworm),
the end of the thread is
located and it is reeled off.
The cocoons remain
bouncing in hot water during
the process as this facilitates
reeling. It is not a very kind
process for the hands of the
women involved. Though the
process is now mechanised,
silk reelers still have to find
the end of the thread in the
hot water before they can
attach it to a mechanical
bobbin.

翠屏放牛

52 'Footprints of a wild swan in the snow'.

6-volume woodcut edition with
illustrations of *Hong xue yin yuan
tu ji* by Linqing, published
between 1847–50.
[15292.f.1 (3).]

Linqing (1791–1846) was a Qing
dynasty official with high family
connections, being a descendant of
the 5th Emperor of the Jin
dynasty (1115–1234) and a family

member of the Imperial
Household Bond-servant Division
of the Manchu Bordered Yellow
Banner. After passing the imperial
civil service exams, he worked as
an official historian and later
served as a prefect in various
different districts before being
appointed Director-General for
River Conservancy in part of

Jiangsu province. He helped to
strengthen the defences of the
northern bank of the Yangtze
River in 1841–2 and wrote several
books on river control, but was
deprived of rank and titles when
the dykes collapsed.

'Footprints of a wild swan in
the snow' contains accounts of 240
incidents in Linqing's life, with

illustrations by his artist-secretaries. The incidents described range from his visits to famous mountains and gardens to descriptions of the river conservancy work and accounts of conversations about chrysanthemums and celebratory dinners in osmanthus groves. The 'unwilling cow' in this illustration had escaped from its owner who intended to slaughter it that day and arrived at the provincial government office like a petitioner with a grievance. Linqing paid the owner for the cow and set it free on a mountain.

53 The West lake at Hangzhou.

Woodblock edition of *Xi Hu jia hua* (Stories of the West Lake), Da wen tang, (n.p.) *c.* 1850.
[15276.b.4.]

The West Lake at Hangzhou has long been famed as one of China's most beautiful tourist centres. It has ancient poetic associations. The lake itself, with wooded banks concealing large temples, studded with landscaped islands, has always been a favourite site for the Chinese. Every temple, island, rock and pool has some story associated with it. Consequently, such books as this, with its map-like illustrations and collection of legends, were very popular with Chinese tourists of the 19th century.

At the top right-hand corner is depicted the Pagoda of Six Harmonies, which still stands. It was first built in 970, to serve as a lighthouse for river traffic and also to protect the town – the river is famous for its high 'bore' tides. Pagodas were originally Indian Buddhist buildings but came to form a distinctive part of the Chinese landscape. According to traditional beliefs about nature and

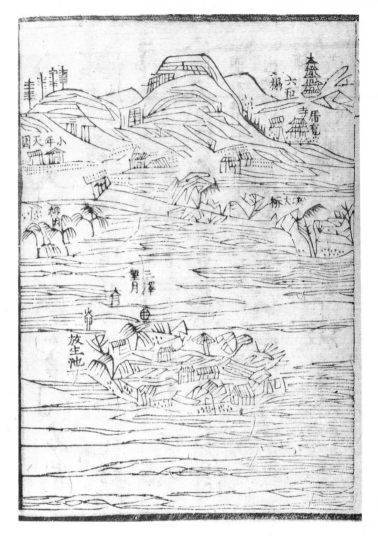

natural forces, local disasters could be averted by building a pagoda on a prominent hill, thereby re-adjusting natural balance. Such pagodas can still be seen dotted about the Chinese countryside.

Suggestions for further reading

SOREN EDGREN *Chinese rare books in American collections* New York, China Institute in America, 1984

DENIS TWITCHETT *Printing and publishing in medieval China* London, Wynken de Worde Society, 1983

THOMAS FRANCIS CARTER *The invention of printing in China and its spread westward* (revised by L. C. Goodrich) New York, Ronald Press, 1955

JOSEPH VEDLICH *The prints of the ten bamboo studio . . .* Fribourg, Productions Libre and Geneva, Editions Minerva, 1979

MAI-MAI SZE *The Tao of painting . . . with a translation of the Mustard Seed garden manual of painting* (2nd ed.) Princeton, Princeton University Press, 1967

T. C. LAI *Chinese decorated letter-paper* Hong Kong, Swindon Book Company, 1978

JEAN MULLIGAN (trans.) *The Lute: Kao Ming's Pi pa ji* New York, Columbia University Press, 1980

C. H. BREWITT-TAYLOR (transl.) *Lo Kuan-chung's Romance of the Three Kingdoms* Rutland, Vermont, Tuttle, 1970

ANTHONY C. YU (transl.) *The Journey to the West* Chicago and London, University of Chicago Press, 1977

DAVID HAWKES (transl.) *The Story of the Stone* (Alternative title for the Dream of the Red Chamber), Harmondsworth, Penguin Books, 1973

T. C. LAI *Ch'i Pai Shih* (on the painter Qi Baishi) Seattle, University of Washington Press, 1973

CRAIG CLUNAS *Chinese Export Watercolours* London, Victoria and Albert Museum, 1984